HISTORIC
COMMUNITIES

A One-Room School

Bobbie Kalman

Toronto · Oxford · New York

Crabtree Publishing Company

HISTORIC COMMUNITIES

Created by Bobbie Kalman

For Jeanette Sorokolit,
with thanks for getting me
through my teenage years

Editor-in-Chief
Bobbie Kalman

Researcher
Lynda Hale

Writing team
Bobbie Kalman
Lynda Hale
David Schimpky
Tammy Everts

Editors
Tammy Everts
David Schimpky
Petrina Gentile
Lynda Hale

Computer design
Lynda Hale

Illustrators
Antoinette "Cookie" DeBiasi
Barb Bedell
Debra Watton
Tammy Everts

Color separations
Book Art Inc.

Special thanks to
Scott Adamson and the staff at the Genesee
Country Museum, Leah Kingston and her
class, and Black Creek Pioneer Village

Published by
Crabtree Publishing Company

350 Fifth Avenue	360 York Road, RR 4	73 Lime Walk
Suite 3308	Niagara-on-the-Lake	Headington
New York	Ontario, Canada	Oxford OX3 7AD
N.Y. 10118	L0S 1J0	United Kingdom

Cataloging in Publication Data
Kalman, Bobbie, 1947-
    A one-room school

(Historic communities series)
Includes index.
ISBN 0-86505-497-5 (library bound) ISBN 0-86505-517-3 (pbk.)
This book examines the daily routine of the one-room school and
includes stories and activities.

1. Rural schools - Juvenile literature. I. Title. II. Series:
Kalman, Bobbie, 1947-   . Historic communities series.

LB1567.K35 1994   j370.19'346   LC 94-5133

Contents

The schoolhouse

It may be difficult to believe, but there was a time when few communities had schools. Children were taught at home, at a neighbor's house, or received no education at all. When a community grew and there were a number of children in an area, the settlers gathered together and built a schoolhouse. With hard work and cooperation, a log schoolhouse could be built quickly.

The first schools

Early schoolhouses had four walls and a roof. One or two windows allowed in just enough sunlight for students to see their work. Long, slanting shelves were attached to the two side walls. These shelves served as desks. Children sat on three-legged stools or simple benches. The teacher's desk, made of rough planks, faced the students. The fireplace barely kept the classroom warm in the winter.

Later schools

As more families sent their children to school, a larger building was needed. The new school had two entrances—one for the girls and one for the boys. Proper desks were purchased to replace the shelves and benches. The girls sat on one side of the room, and the boys on the other. The youngest children sat at the front of the classroom, close to the teacher. Behind the teacher was a blackboard. A wood stove heated the classroom.

Children of all ages were taught in the same classroom. What do you think the boy wearing the dunce cap did to deserve his punishment?

The teacher rules!

To become a teacher, a man or woman had to be able to read, write, and handle rough-and-ready students. Most teachers were men. They were called **schoolmasters**. Female teachers had to be single. Once a woman married, she was not allowed to continue teaching in the school.

Hiring the teacher

When a new teacher arrived in town, he or she was given food and shelter. Every family in the community paid a small amount of money for the teacher's salary and took turns boarding the teacher. The families that could not pay with money gave the teacher goods such as corn or tobacco. The goods were then traded for money or other items at the general store.

Early teachers did not have the special training that teachers have today. Many male teachers were retired soldiers who knew how to read and write and needed a job after leaving the army.

The teacher shown in the above picture would never have been hired in settler times. Do you know why? See the caption on page 28 for the answer.

Teaching the children

One teacher instructed all the children in the
school. He or she taught as many as eight grades
at a time. The class was divided into four groups,
each with an upper and lower grade. If there
were many children in a community, only the
older students were allowed to attend school
during the school year. A female teacher was
hired to teach the younger children during the
summer months.

Keeping order in the classroom

The teacher did more than teach the children.
He or she also had to keep order in the school.
With children of all ages learning different things
at the same time, good behavior was important.
It was the responsibility of the teacher to punish
children who misbehaved.

*(left) A female teacher was rare.
Women were required to quit their
teaching job once they married.*

*(right) After the students went
home, the teacher made sure the
classroom was tidy for the next day.*

The three Rs

Teachers rarely had enough time to teach more than three subjects. The three subjects, or the "three Rs," of early education were reading, writing, and arithmetic—or "reading, 'riting, and 'rithmetic."

Learning the basics

Most of the settlers were religious. They wanted to be able to read because it was believed that a person who could read the Bible would become a better Christian. Good **penmanship** was also considered a valuable skill. Neat handwriting was thought to be the sign of a cultured person. Knowing how to write and **cipher**, or do arithmetic, was important for anyone who wanted to be a farmer, storekeeper, craftsperson, or miller.

*Arithmetic was taught by **drill**. Children learned to add, subtract, multiply, and divide by solving problems in their head. They had to know the answers as soon as the teacher flashed the cards.*

Memorizing and reciting

Schoolbooks and writing paper were scarce in settler times. Students did much of their learning by **rote**, which meant memorizing long poems and stories and reciting them to the teacher. Students also had to write and deliver speeches.

A better education

Some larger schools taught more than the "three Rs." At these schools, students learned grammar, history, and geography. During grammar lessons, students learned how to **parse** sentences. Parsing means explaining the meaning and function of each word in a sentence. History lessons concentrated on events that had taken place in North America. In geography class, students memorized the names of countries, capital cities, lakes, rivers, and mountains. If the school had a globe, the teacher spun it so fast that it became a colorful blur. He or she suddenly stopped the spinning globe and pointed to a location to be named by the students.

quill pen and inkwell

(left) Students practiced drawing slants and pothooks for hours. Being able to draw straight lines and smooth curves was an important part of beautiful penmanship.

(right) Reading aloud was a good way to learn pronunciation and grammar.

School supplies

Can you imagine going to a school that does not have supplies such as notebooks, pencils, markers, paints, scissors, and textbooks? Few of these things were available to settler school children. The supplies they used were very different from those used in schools today.

Books, books, books

The early schools had only two books for students: the Bible and a **primer**. Much of the school day was devoted to memorizing and reciting verses from the Bible. The primer contained the alphabet, numbers, spelling words, and poems. It was used by students who were beginning to learn how to read and write. Some students also used **hornbooks**. A hornbook was a wooden paddle with a piece of paper on it that showed letters, numbers, and Bible verses. A thin, transparent layer of horn protected the paper from damage.

a hornbook

McGuffey Readers

The most popular readers of the nineteenth century were the *Eclectic Readers* by William Holmes McGuffey. This set of six readers began with a primer. Each volume increased in difficulty. Children in the one-room school advanced through the readers at their own pace. Not only did the McGuffey Readers teach children how to read, they also taught values such as honesty, courage, charity, and good manners.

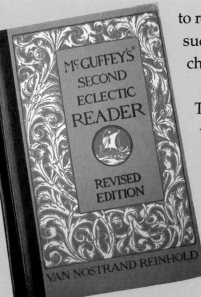

The McGuffey Readers were first published in 1836, and more than 122 million copies of the readers were sold by the 1920s. In some areas only the Bible was more popular than the McGuffey Reader.

By the late nineteenth century a wide variety of textbooks had been published on spelling, grammar, arithmetic, geography, and history. Unfortunately, few communities could afford textbooks for every student.

Copybooks and slates

Children in early schools practiced writing in **copybooks**. Today notebook paper is lined but, in the early schools, copybook paper was blank. Using a ruler, the students had to draw straight lines in their books. Students who could not afford copybooks practiced writing on **slates**, which were like small blackboards. Children used slate pencils to write on these boards.

Quills

Settler students did not have pens as we have today. Instead, they dipped sharpened goose feathers, called **quills**, in ink. Keeping quill pens sharp was one of the duties of the teacher, but sometimes this job was done by responsible, older students. Writing with a quill pen left a lot of wet ink on a page. To prevent smudging, students covered the page with **blotting paper** after they finished writing. They pressed the paper down on the page to absorb the extra ink.

Slates and pencils were made of hard rock. Students wrote by scratching the slate with their pencils. After several years, a slate was covered with hundreds of scratches. Modern chalk is much gentler on blackboards!

Running the school

The schoolhouse was a source of community pride. Everyone did his or her share to keep it in good order. Although part of the teacher's job was keeping the school clean, much of the work was done by the students.

Keep the fire burning

Early schools were cold in the winter! The only source of heat in a one-room school came from a wood stove located in the center of the room. Some families supplied the school with wood for the stove. The children had to walk to school carrying an armful of firewood. Each morning a different child was responsible for starting the fire before the other children arrived.

(left) Families in the community took turns sending wood to school with the children. This boy is starting the fire to warm up the classroom before the other children arrive.

*(right) A **yoke** was used for fetching heavy buckets of drinking water from the well.*

Cleaning the schoolhouse

Keeping the schoolhouse clean was not an easy job. The teacher had to ensure that the chimney was clear of soot so the class would not be "smoked out." Each day the floors were swept and the blackboards cleaned. The windows of the school, which allowed in the only light in the room, needed frequent washing.

Helping the teacher

The teacher assigned chores to the students. Most children enjoyed helping. When a fresh supply of drinking water was needed, it was a chance to take a stroll outside. The wonders of nature often distracted the water fetcher! Not all children were willing workers, however. Sometimes the teacher assigned chores as a punishment!

(left) At the end of each day, the blackboards had to be washed.

(right) On cold winter mornings, students were thankful that the stove was already warm when they entered the school.

John cared for his sick calf before leaving for school.

Getting to school

Getting to school was not easy for many settler children. The school was often a long way from home. Most children had to walk, but there were other ways of getting to school.

John's trip to school

John's feet dragged as he began the long walk to the schoolhouse. He had been awake since daybreak, when he started his chores. He spied his friend Philip walking ahead of him. "Philip!" he shouted. "Wait up!"

Philip waited until John caught up with him. John told him about a sick calf at the farm. Philip showed John his new slingshot.

"Can I give it a try?" asked John. Philip nodded, and John aimed at a squirrel. PING! The stone bounced off a tree. The two boys laughed at the poor shot. John was having so much fun that he soon forgot how tired he was.

Just then, John and Philip heard the clip-clop of a horse's hoofs behind them. They turned around and spotted the Johnson twins, who were riding an old mare to school. The two boys smiled and waved at the twins.

Moments later, John's Uncle Dan came by on his wagon. "Want a ride, boys?" he asked.

"Sure," replied John and Philip. They were happy to avoid the rest of the walk. Uncle Dan told them that he thought cold weather was on its way. John was not at all pleased with this prediction. The long walk to school was even worse in winter! Sudden blizzards made it

Philip walked slowly, waiting for his friend John to catch up with him.

impossible to see where he was going. Walking through the snow froze his toes. Sometimes he stuffed straw in his boots to keep out the cold.

Uncle Dan laughed when John complained about winter. "Don't worry, my boy. Just be at this spot every morning and I'll pick you up in my sleigh on my way to town."

John was very happy to hear this generous offer. Perhaps winter wouldn't be so bad after all!

Daily routine

A daily routine helped the teacher keep order in the busy classroom. This schedule also ensured that the students learned as much as possible.

(above) Since students shared the same classroom for as many as eight years, they heard the lessons of other classes year after year. They remembered these lessons long after they finished school!

(below) It was difficult to work when the room was filled with the screeching and scratching of slate pencils against slates.

School's in!
The ringing of the teacher's bell signaled the beginning of the school day. As the children entered the school, they "made their manners," bowing and curtsying to the teacher. Opening exercises began with the Lord's Prayer, Bible readings, and roll call. Anyone who was not present during roll call waited outside until recess—even on bitterly cold winter days!

Getting down to business
The first subjects of the day were reading and writing. Each grade took turns reading aloud while the other students did written work. After recess, the children practiced arithmetic. They

were taught to solve difficult math problems without using a slate and pencil! Afternoons were devoted to special classes such as history, geography, and speech-making.

Another day done!

Each day ended with the teacher's announcements. The duties for the next day were handed out, and the children who misbehaved were kept late. The rest of the students were dismissed in an orderly fashion, often marching out of the room to a beat rapped on the desk by the teacher. Chatter filled the schoolyard as the students left the building.

(above) Outside the entrance to the schoolhouse, the children formed a straight line from youngest to oldest. If the school had two entrances, as this school did, the boys lined up at one door and the girls at the other.

(top left) Each morning the students "made their manners" to the teacher.

(bottom left) Saying the Lord's Prayer was a part of the morning opening exercises.

Lunchtime

Each morning students walked to school swinging their lunch baskets and tin pails. Their lunches often included homemade bread smothered with jam. Donuts were a tasty treat —if they didn't get mushed in the lunchpail! Some children brought pie for dessert. Most pies were like turnovers with thick crusts and juicy fruit filling.

Growing food for lunch

Tending the school garden was a practical way to learn about nature and grow food for lunch at the same time. Each child was responsible for a small plot of land. Some children combined their plots to create larger ones.

Students learned how plants grew, and they tried different ways to make seeds grow faster. Most students grew root vegetables, such as carrots and turnips, which could be stored for the winter. During cold weather, a team of children was responsible for making vegetable soup in the schoolhouse. Everyone shared the hot, nutritious soup and helped clean up afterwards.

Mmm…hot chocolate!

At some schools, children took turns bringing a pail of milk to school each day. At lunchtime they placed the bucket of milk on the stove. Students looked forward to having hot cocoa with their lunch. Sometimes they forgot to loosen the lid of the pail, which caused an explosion that sent scalding milk flying to the ceiling! Fortunately, these accidents rarely occurred.

Working in the school garden taught children skills they would need as farmers.

In the wintertime many students carried half-baked potatoes to school. The potatoes, which had been heated before the children left for school, kept little hands warm during the long, cold walk. Students finished cooking the potatoes on the wood stove at school. Do you think these two children have potatoes hidden under the cloths covering their hands?

Recess

Students had a short recess break in the morning and afternoon. They rushed outdoors to play games, talk, or explore the nearby woods.

Homemade toys

Settler children made many of their recess toys from items they found at home or in town. Yarn that came from old unravelled sweaters was rolled into balls for playing catch. Thick twigs were carved into whistles. Barrel staves became the runners of speedy sleds called **skipjacks**. When large farm animals were slaughtered, their bladders were washed and blown up. Children used these bladders as balloons or footballs!

*(left) String games were played by most settler children. Some, such as **Cat's Cradle**, are still played today.*

(right) Tottering atop tall stilts was an activity only for the brave and sure-footed.

Games

Playing with marbles was a popular pastime. Children competed to win the most "aggies," "cat-eyes," and "bosses." Older girls, who were not allowed to participate in lively games, played guessing games with beans, buttons, and string. Younger children enjoyed singing games such as "Ring Around the Rosy" and "Farmer in the Dell."

Early chewing gum

What we call gum today is actually a mixture of sugar and artificial ingredients. Settler school children chewed real gum that came from spruce or balsam trees. After the hardened sap was warmed in the mouth, it became chewy and had a strong taste that was very different from the flavor of today's bubble gum.

(left) A spinning toy called a **whirligig** *can be made using a few pieces of wood and some string.*

(right) A wooden toy called an **acrobat** *was popular with settler children.*

21

Pranks and jokes

This teacher is not amused by her snowy likeness. The boys in the bushes are laughing at their joke now, but will they be laughing later?

Settler children had very little time for play. Chores, traveling to and from school, and studies took up most of the day. Children used every opportunity to laugh and play. They often pulled tricks and pranks on one another. Many children became expert pranksters, especially at school!

What a joke!

A common practical joke at the one-room school was called "smoking out the master." A group of older boys would climb onto the roof of the schoolhouse and cover the chimney with branches. The classroom soon filled with smoke, and everyone was forced to run outside!

Older children played pranks on younger children. Imagine a child's surprise when he or she opened a pencil box to find a jumping grasshopper, a spindly spider, or a gopher's tail! Screams and cries for help were always signs of a successful prank.

The raw materials

School supplies provided endless amusement! Children used blotting paper to make spitballs. Bottles, which contained water to clean slates, were tipped over to wet the seats of classmates who were reciting at the front of the room.

(right) "Smoking out the master" was a dangerous practical joke.

23

Dreaded punishments

Pranksters tried to avoid being caught by the teacher because punishments could be harsh. Boys and girls were disciplined for arriving late, answering questions incorrectly, and falling asleep in class. Besides being punished at school, children were usually punished again when they returned home!

These two boys enjoyed playing their pranks but are not as happy with their punishments. One has to balance on a block, and the other was told to put on a bonnet and sit on the girl's side of the classroom.

Lines, dunce caps, and the rod

"Bad" behavior led to any one of a number of punishments. Sometimes children were ordered to memorize long passages or write lines over and over. Teachers also shamed their students by making them wear a "dunce cap" or a sign around their neck. Some students were forced to balance on a block of wood in a corner of the classroom. One of the most common punishments was getting a whipping with a hickory switch or a birch rod. Sometimes the strapping was so severe that students went home with red marks across their legs.

Writing lines was a gentle form of punishment, but it certainly wasn't any fun! Students copied the same sentence hundreds of times.

Standing on end

The mere threat of "the peg" was enough to change any child's behavior! The guilty pupil's hair was fastened to a clip, which was pegged into the wall at a height that kept the child standing on tiptoes until the teacher thought the student had learned his or her lesson.

Don't spare the rod!

When boys fought in the classroom, the punishment didn't come from the teacher. After he or she separated the scrapping boys, each was given a beech rod and told to "lay on and cut jackets." The boys had to flog one another! If they didn't hit hard enough, they received a stinging lash from the teacher. The students soon learned that fighting was not acceptable behavior!

Having to wear a "dunce cap" was a humiliating punishment.

Special events

Every Friday, school ended with a **spell-down**, or **spelling bee**. Two of the older students picked teams. The children took turns spelling words that were read aloud by the teacher. If someone misspelled a word, he or she was out of the game and had to sit down. The bee ended when only one person was left standing. The winner was a school celebrity until the next spelling bee. Everyone admired the person who could "spell down" the entire school.

Sometimes spelling bees were held for everyone in the community. During the long winter evenings, a spelling match was a great opportunity to gather with friends and neighbors and test one's language skills.

In some communities, an adult who had an ear for music held singing school at night. Singing and spending time with friends made for a fun evening.

The Christmas pageant

The Christmas pageant was one of the biggest events of the year! The entire community packed into the decorated schoolhouse to watch the children perform math drills, songs, poetry readings, and plays. Often the older boys and girls gave a special presentation or play that they had written and prepared on their own. Children spent months getting ready for the pageant. It was a chance for them to demonstrate the skills they had learned throughout the year.

School's out!

Near the end of the school year the students were given an oral examination by the teacher. Students had to spell, solve arithmetic problems, and answer questions on a variety of subjects. Parents and villagers were an eager audience. The day after their "exams," the children breathed a sigh of relief and took part in a community picnic. Both children and adults participated in races and other outdoor games. Afterwards, everyone sat down to enjoy a delicious lunch.

A favorite Christmas story was Charles Dickens's **A Christmas Carol.** *It was often performed as a play during Christmas pageants.*

The last day of school was a happy occasion for feasting, games, and dancing.

Locked in school!

Amanda draws happily on her slate. When the teacher finds out she is left-handed, she will certainly be forced to write with her right hand. In settler times, left-handed people were thought to be "bad!"

Amanda had never been to school before, and everything puzzled her. When the teacher asked her to spell "frog," she didn't know what spelling meant. She drew a picture on her slate instead. The concerned teacher, Miss Crabtree, wanted to test Amanda's skills, so she told her to stay after school.

The other children stared at Amanda and snickered. At recess they told her she would be punished for drawing instead of spelling. Amanda grew more and more worried as the day went on. Her heart sank when the teacher dismissed all the students—except her.

As the class filed out of the one-room school, the students chattered happily with one another. The sounds in the schoolyard gradually grew fainter until they disappeared entirely.

Just after the children left, a man came and spoke to Miss Crabtree. She followed him outside and shut the door behind her. Amanda waited. She wondered how long it would be before the teacher returned to punish her. Mother had a watermelon waiting at home, and Amanda could almost taste its ripe, juicy lusciousness. A tear rolled down her cheek. Perhaps this was her punishment—to be left alone in this huge, bare room with flies humming in lazy circles near the ceiling. She felt frightened and abandoned.

"Just after the children left, a man came and spoke to Miss Crabtree."

In the meantime, Amanda's mother and Aunt Cordelia wondered why it was taking Amanda so long to get home from school. "Amanda is never late," said Aunt Cordelia. Amanda's mother decided to start searching for her daughter. She stopped at the neighbors' houses to see if Amanda had gone home with one of the other children, but Amanda was nowhere to be found. She then headed in the direction of the house where Miss Crabtree lived.

When the schoolteacher heard that Amanda had not gone home, she suddenly remembered asking the little girl to stay after school. She blushed when she realized that she had completely forgotten about her pupil. Could Amanda still be waiting at the school?

By the time Amanda's mother and the teacher arrived at the school, it was dark. Miss Crabtree carried a lantern inside and found Amanda sitting up straight at her desk, her cheeks streaked with tears.

When Amanda saw her mother, she cried and pointed to the teacher. "Miss Crabtree told me to stay!" Mother held poor Amanda as she sobbed. The teacher was very embarrassed and offered to give Amanda extra help after school—but not at the schoolhouse. Amanda would be tutored at her own home.

"We've saved you a big piece of watermelon," Mother said to Amanda, who smiled. From that moment on, that was all she could think about! No longer angry, Amanda asked the teacher to dinner.

Alone in the schoolhouse, Amanda waits for someone to remember her.

Games and activities

Many teachers used songs and rhymes to teach grammar, spelling, and arithmetic. Try the following problems, quizzes, and games and decide if they make learning more fun!

First and last letters

How many words do you know that begin with the letter "t" and end with the letter "m?" Ask your friends to write down as many of these words as they can. As each list is read aloud, everyone checks off the same words from his or her list. Players score one point for each word that the other players did not have. Change the first and last letters until someone scores 25 points.

Nonsense numbering

The following rhyme is one way to count to ten. Use it to solve the problem below.

Onery, twoery, fithery, sithery, san, Wheelerbone, whackerbone, inery, ninery, tan

Sam has saved fithery pennies to buy candies to surprise his twoery friends. The shopkeeper tells Sam that he can purchase fithery licorice for onery penny and sithery candy drops for onery penny. If Sam spends all his money on licorice and candy drops and his purchase includes wheelerbone licorice, how many candy drops did Sam buy?

Here today, gone tomorrow!

The following list describes some of the daily activities that took place in the one-room school. Divide a page into two columns. In one column, name the activities that occurred **only** in the settler school; in the other, list the activities that still occur in schools today.

- if you misbehave in class, you must wear a dunce cap
- "make your manners" to your teacher every morning
- help with routine chores such as cleaning the blackboards
- study the three Rs, history, geography, and other subjects
- write neatly with quill pens and ink
- begin school when the bell rings
- learn lessons with children of all ages in one classroom
- take a morning and afternoon recess break
- play games such as hide-and-seek, leap frog, or dodge ball during breaks

In your opinion, have schools improved over the years? Why or why not?

(above) The students in this picture made a model of a settler farm. They also spent a day being students in a one-room settler school. What object can you find in this modern classroom that you could not find in a settler school?

(opposite page) The one-room school had strict rules, but most children loved going to it just the same.

31

Glossary

artificial Something made by people that does not occur in nature

bladder A sac in the body that stores fluid

blizzard A severe snowstorm

blotting paper Soft paper used to absorb extra ink

board To provide meals and a place to stay

cipher To do simple arithmetic

craftsperson A skilled person who makes goods by hand

flog To beat or whip

grammar The study of the proper use of language

horn A thin, transparent substance that comes from the horn of an animal

marbles Small glass balls that are used in games

oral examination A test in which questions and answers are given aloud

pageant A special event or show

penmanship The quality or style of handwriting

pothooks The curves of letters made by children learning to write

prankster A person who plays tricks or pranks

recite To repeat aloud from memory

roll call The reading aloud of a list of names to determine who is present

slaughter To kill animals for food

stave A long, curved piece of wood that forms the side of a barrel

switch A slender stick or rod used for whipping

Index

Acknowledgments

Photo credits
Jim Bryant: page 6
Marc Crabtree: pages 7 (right), 10, 11 (both), 12 (right), 13 (left), 14, 17 (right), 19, 21 (left)
Peter Crabtree: page 9 (left)
Ken Faris: page 25 (top)
Bobbie Kalman: title page, pages 7 (left), 8, 9 (right), 12 (left), 13 (right), 16, 17 (top, bottom), 25 (bottom), 31
Metropolitan Regional Conservation Authority: pages 18, 20 (both), 21 (right), 27, 30

Illustrations and colorizations
Antoinette "Cookie" DeBiasi: title page, pages 9, 10, 14, 15, 16, 19, 22, 23 (right), 26 (bottom), 27, 28, 29 (both)
Barb Bedell: cover, pages 4-5
Debra Watton: page 24
Tammy Everts: pages 23 (left), 25 (both), 26 (top)

4 5 6 7 8 9 0   Printed in U.S.A.   3 2 1 0 9 8 7 6 5